Microcosm is Portland's autistic-founded, worker-owned, and most diversified publishing house and distributor with a focus on the colorful, authentic, and empowering. Our books and zines have put your power in your hands since 1996, equipping readers to make positive changes in their lives and in the world around them. Microcosm emphasizes skill-building, showing hidden histories, and fostering creativity through challenging conventional publishing wisdom with books and bookettes about DIY skills, food, bicycling, gender, self-care, and social justice.

contents...

CALL ME *Brenda*

My name is Mary Beth and I am a Customer Service Representative. I am the cheerful voice at the other end of the toll free customer support 800 number. Customers often mess up my name, which is fine. I don't take it personally. I'm not surprised when they substitute "Mary Beth" with another Mary combo - Mary Ann, Mary Jo, Mary Sue, Mary Alice, etc. However, a lot of customers - A LOT of customers - call me Brenda. After confusing me for some random Mary combo name, Brenda is the number one wrong name I'm called. I have no idea why. I don't really notice it that much anymore, but every now and then it does make me consider what my life would've been like had I been named Brenda. It's something to think about.

I've been at this job for five years. Working at a call center was never a career goal of mine, but it's not that bad. I work from home and I make a surprisingly decent amount of money. I get a lot of paid time off and really, really good benefits. I can get an MRI for twenty dollars… I mean, that's almost the same as going to the movies. I do have to talk to angry customers... but then there are those twenty dollar MRI's.

I talk to an average of thirty to forty people a day. The disembodied voices of thirty to forty random people from all over the U.S. I picture our conversations like little clouds or bubbles floating over the country. When we hang up, the cloud dissolves or the bubble pops. When I'm not at work and I look at the sky, I imagine a bunch of complaint-filled clouds and/or bubbles. It's really not a very poetic thought - all of America's grievances hanging above us. There have to be some consequences to us filling the atmosphere with our whiny, frustrated, loney, entitled and angry sentiments. I feel like we're feeling those consequences now... and I feel like I should say something profound about empathy being necessary for awareness and how a society fueled by self interest and greed can never muster the compassion necessaray to save itself before it's too late. But that's depressing and makes me sound, and feel, pretentious and annoying. Eh... so here's some stuff about talking to customers all day, many who happen to call me Brenda.

Call log

7:03 am Carol from Phenix City, Alabama has to keep close tabs on her adult son. She assigned a ringtone to him that sounds like a baby crying.

8:12 am Sam from Vermillion, South Dakota did not believe I could do math. He made me repeat each step of my calculations while he followed along and was annoyed when it ended up that I was correct.

8:40 am Ken from Pocatello, Idaho was concerned about account security. His teenage daughter hacked his online account and reset her data limits. I reset Ken's online password. He is hopeful this will slow her down.

9:26 am Amanda from Merrillville, Indiana is just disappointed.

9:40 am April from Cyril, Oklahoma doesn't have enough money to get a replacement phone for her husband. She doesn't know what they are going to do.

10:08 am Sheila from Griffin, Georgia is a snowbird and needed me to update her winter address. She needed proof of her new address to renew her driver's license.

10:12 am Khanhi from Altadena, California wants a lower bill. Her husband is having surgery and she feels like a single mom. She told me I would have good karma because I took care of my parents when they were old. She assured me that, even though I don't have kids, someone will take care of me when I'm old.

10:25 am Jessica from Wray, Georgia finally called in about her mom's account. Her mom died in December and had lived with her for the past ten years.

11:44 am Gina from La Union, New Mexico uses her mobile hotspot for work and thinks her computer has a virus.

12:06 pm Lydia from Santa Clara, Utah was in a hurry and didn't hang up at the end of our call. I overheard several minutes of her conversation with a coworker. It wasn't very interesting.

AUGUST 4, 2020

12:44 pm Doris from Franklin Lakes, New Jersey called to make sure her autopay was set up and her expired card was taken off her account. She was mean and kept saying that she shouldn't have to call about this. She wanted to be credited for her time. She said that I was pathetic and a dumb machine could do my job. To demonstrate she shouted, "Hey Google! Cancel!" three times. She eventually asked for a supervisor and I transferred her.

12:59 pm Fatuma from Mesa, Arizona was yelling at her children during the call. She told them if they said any more bad words they would go into time out.

1:23 pm Sean from San Bernardino, California changes his phone number a lot. He gets harassing phone calls.

1:54 pm Shelli from Fort Myers, Florida was very upset that I couldn't give her a way to contact me directly. I did not fix the problem that she called in about and I don't care.

2:19 pm James from Gorham, New Hampshire was very chatty. We talked about Nebraska and tornadoes.

2:40 pm Louis from Middleburg, Florida seemed genuinely concerned about my well being. When I asked him how he was doing, he said, "And you, you okay?" It sounded like he cared.

2:53 pm Frances from Brownsville, Texas is scared of the internet.

3:02 pm Jimmy from Martin, Georgia was very nervous and did not want to trouble me by asking too many questions.

3:12 pm Darren from Moriarty, New Mexico called about an app on his phone. He told me that he is tired of Covid and can't wait for it to be over. He speculated about various pandemic conspiracy theories involving the government. He told me that "blessings of the Higher Almighty will come down upon you." He also told me to "have a blessing day." He blessed me over ten times.

MY CUSTOMER SERVICE

Nobody calls customer service because they're happy. So not surprisingly, people's behavior on the phone is only one step above an online comment section… it gets a bit nasty. But I have two secret weapons, or Customer Service Superpowers - a cheerful, freakishly childlike voice and well-honed passive aggressiveness.

I have the voice of a twelve year old girl, really high and really young sounding. It usually disarms angry customers. Nobody wants to yell at a twelve year old girl. Or at least most people. It can work against me, though. Customers, frequently male customers, don't take me seriously or believe what I'm telling them. A couple of customers have even asked to be transferred to a guy. Since we do not have a "Man Customer Service Rep"

Taming the cobra…

September 15, 2020, 2:53 pm
Joanne from Chappaqua, New York called because she was very angry at the tech support representative she spoke with the previous night. She said he was condescending and she felt like he wasn't concerned about her problem. I told her that nothing makes me more angry than when someone talks to me like I'm stupid. We chatted a bit and she calmed down. She shared that she had lost four people to Covid. I can't imagine what that would be like. At the end of the call she said, "Mary Beth, when we get off this call, you take a moment and congratulate yourself because you have tamed a cobra. When I am angry I am a cobra and nobody can stop me. But you calmed me down. You tamed a cobra."

Superpower!

department, I transfer them to other random companies like Geico, Wells Fargo, or Pottery Barn, etc. Maybe they'll end up getting a male representative, maybe they won't. Not my problem.

I'm from the Midwest so the passive aggressiveness comes naturally. We are masters at deflecting, avoiding and repressing all things uncomfortable or unpleasant.

Confrontation you say? Oooooh no. No, no, no. Just let me tell you about this shiny thing over here, slip in a few quick jabs that you don't really notice, then give you a sloppy verbal hug, comment on how great your garden looks this year (what?!) and how smart your kid is, and then send you on your way. Was I dishonest? No. Do I really know anything about your garden? No. Is your kid smart? I don't know. (Probably not, judging from the fact that you're calling in because you just noticed a $10 charge on your bill that's been on there every month for the last year...)

I told you the truth - that you've been paying $10 a month for that useless piece of equipment the salesperson fast talked you into buying. I also made a semi-snide comment about reading things before you sign them, but that went waaaaay over your Go-Go-Go-Get-It-Done-Now-Now-Now-And-Let-Me-Tell-You-Another-Thing-East-Coast head. Then I tied it all up with a funny personal anecdote and a pathetically small discount. Everyone leaves happy.

I try hard to be upfront, honest and as non-scammy with my customers as possible. But if someone's being a jerk, I'll do what I have to do to get off that call without saying something that will get me fired. If the customer ends up happy or mildly satisfied... well, fantastic!

Rat love

September 14, 2020, 9:00 a.m.

Stephen from Philadelphia, Pennsylvannia called in last week about adding a tablet or wireless notebook to his account. He was a really neat guy. He had a vet emergency, though, and we ended the call abruptly.

I called back today and found out that his vet emergency turned out to be for one of his rats. He runs a rat rescue shelter… like for stray dogs, but for rats instead. Apparently rat shelters are pretty common. I was excited to talk to someone with rat knowledge and asked him a ton of questions. My wife wants a pet rat and I want reasons why we should not get one. We also talked about cults and art. He was really funny and I wish we could be friends. I hope his rats are okay.

Over twenty years ago

September 20, 2020, 10:20 a.m.

Dianne from Mesa, Arizona called because the alarm on her phone stopped working. She was 84 years old and had a foul mouth. We started talking about the weather and she said, "I can't even open the fucking door. My husband has dementia and he'll just wander off in his wheelchair." She went on to say, "He's been a quad [quadrapalegic] since '91 and was supposed to die within five years. Well that was over twenty years ago and now he has dementia. What the fuck do I do now?" There was a pause then we both started laughing. We laughed so hard we couldn't talk for over three straight minutes, which is an eternity in call center time.

my happy place

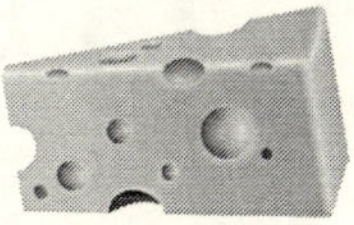

These are some of the things I look at when I want to stab a pen in my eye. So far it's been an effective deterrent... I still have two functioning eyes.

SURVEY SAYS!

Question 1: On a scale of one to five, with one being the lowest and five being the highest, how would you rate Mary Beth's performance?
Question 2: On a scale of one to five, with one being the lowest and five being the highest, how would you rate Randomcorp based on your experience with Mary Beth?

September 1, 2020 Shavina, Greenville, South Carolina
Q1: 5 She was pleasant, personable, helpful, efficient
Q2: 5 I got the help I needed

September 1, 2020 Maria, Appleton, Wisconsin
Q1: 5 Mary Beth was very friendly and went out of her way to provide excellent customer service in resolving my issues.
Q2: 5 My customer service experience with Mary Beth gave me a great impression of Randomcorp and how it values its customers.

September 2, 2020 Daniel, Newton, Massachusetts
Q1: 5 Patient, down to earth, good strong voice that can I hear. I can't hear people with high pitch voices. Polite and just a pleasant person. For the record I do not like most people I talk to about problems cause it sometimes seems I am bothering them. They make me madder than I was originally.
Q2: 5 You promote autopay by giving better deals. Instead you should be giving the deals to customers who have been with you for many years and have a great payment record. Consider plans for people that are in low paying jobs. A person that has not missed a payment in all these years and has a great credit score is so much more apt to pay their bill that an auto pay person cause if the money is not there autopay cannot get it. An autopay person can let a credit card go bad in hard times. I have been paying my bill longer than many of your employees have worked there. But your young executives think they know better. Have a great day and God bless you.

Customers receive after-call surveys via text message. The first question they're asked is, "On a scale of one to five, with one being the lowest and five being the highest, how would you rate (reps name)'s performance?" Then they're asked, "How would you rate Randomocorp based on your experience with (rep name)?" Customers have a chance to leave comments after each rating. The surveys are sent out randomly. Reps don't know which customers get a survey or respond to one until the results come back. A score of 5 is considered perfect and anything lower is a failed survey.

September 3, 2020 Alejandra, Salinas, California

Q1: 5 She was kind, informative, and expedient in helping me solve my problem

Q2: 5 Because if you had more Mary Beth's working at Randomcorp, I would be a lifelong customer

September 3, 2020 Brian, Cincinnati, Ohio

Q1: 5 Mary Beth was VERY helpful and kind and intelligent. I almost always have bad customer service experiences when I call anywhere. Thank you Mary Beth :)

Q2: 5 Helpful customer service

September 6, 2020 Nolan, Aiken, South Carolina

Q1: 5 She was very polite and pleasant and she promptly took care of my needs and did not try to sell me on something I didn't ask for.

Q2: 5 Good service

September 8, 2020 Robert, Boston, Massachusetts

Q1: 5 She's very smart, to the point, made me feel easy to talk to.

Q2: 5 When I say excellent, that is enough

SURVEY SAYS!, CONT.

September 8, 2020 Shawn, Macon, Georgia

Q1: 5 Because the young lady I had was very pleasant and she explained it me in detail that's why I picked a 5 AWESOME

Q2: 5 Because it's just that a 5 and that's why I'm still a customer

September 8, 20202 Justin, Katy, Texas

Q1: 5 Because she cared she did what she had to do to get my bill lowered and did something that the nine previous representatives we're not able to do [sic].

Q2: 5 Very friendly and easy to talk to, usually I talk to a foreigner but I got an American

September 9, 2020 Caroline, Elizabeth, New Jersey

Q1: 5 She was friendly and patient. She seemed like a nice person. I could understand her clearly (no accent). She was not pushy. I am grateful she was able to help me.

Q2: 4 No thanks

September 9, 2020 Mildred, Scranton, Pennsylvannia

Q1: 5 Brenda was very knowledgeable and very helpful, very pleasant. Much preferred over the automated system. I'd rather pay the money than go through that agony

Q2: 5 Because I got to speak to a real person

September 10, 2020 Allen, Spanish Fork, Utah

Q1: 5 She directed me to someone who could finally help

Q2: 4 I have been so dissatisfied with my phone that otherwise my rating would have been 1

September 10, 2020 Martin, Amherst, Massachusetts

Q1: 5 She was courteous and responsive.

Q2: 4 Received what I needed, but don't need these texts questioning me about it.

September 13, 2020 Neil, Kennesaw, Georgia

Q1: 5 Excellent service. Very good people skills. She is type of a customer service that makes me stay with Randomcorp.

Q2: 5 I love Randomcorp customer service and that they are based in USA, not Asia

September 14, 2020 Bambi, Childress, Texas

Q1: 5 Was accurate

Q2: 2 Don't always get the right answers

September 13, 2020 Cordell, Rincon, Georgia

Q1: 4 Excellent listener and very helpful

Q2: 4 Our goal was achieved efficiently

September 14, 2020 Cindy, Webster, New York

Q1: 5 Last month I spent a long time with a Randomcorp rep getting the right plan and price higher and took care of it, in addition she looked over everything to make sure future bills would be correct

Q2: 5 Again Marybeth went above and beyond. I was ready to switch to another carrier

September 14, 2020 Marquisa, Simpsonville, South Carolina

Q1: 5 Because Ms Mary Beth was polite and she was very helpful as well as patient

Q2: 5 Great!

September 15, 2020 Henry, Auburn, New York

Q1: 4 Mary Beth listened to my concerns and helped me resolve any problems

Q2: 4 There was very little hold time before speaking to a Randomcorp specialist

September 15, 2020 Michael, Leeds, Alabama

Q1: 5 She was knowledgeable, super nice and friendly. She really acted like I wasn't bothering her. Y'all need to clone her

Q2: 5 Because of Mary Beth

SURVEY SAYS!, CONT.

September 15, 2020 Tyronne, Dayton, Ohio

Q1: 5 Mary Beth was very pleasant and knowledgeable, found and corrected my issue quickly

Q2: 5 I'm very satisfied

September 20, 2020 Trisha, Medford, Oregon

Q1: 5 Because she was excellent

Q2: 3 Because it is what it is

September 20, 2020 Dominique, Brooklyn, New York

Q1: 5 Great customer satisfaction

Q2: 5 Beautiful lady

September 20, 2020 Juan, Durango, Colorado

Q1: 5 Extremely helpful and held to her pleasant demeanor even when she could tell I was getting a little annoyed with the situation (nothing to do with her)

Q2: 3 Past issues

September 20, 2020 Isaac, Chester, New Jersey

Q1: 5 Great sense of humor

Q2: 5 Everything was solved

September 21, 2020 Marcia, Snellville, Georgia

Q1: 5 Excellent customer service

Q2: 5 She interacted well and even gave her personal experience

September 21, 2020 Kandace, St. George, Utah

Q1: 5 She has been the best of so many representatives!!!!

Q2: 2 The plans are expensive

September 22, 2020 Manny, Richmond, Virginia

Q1: 5 Delightful and fixed my phone

Q2: 4 Customer service rep was great but the wait and our inability to use the online help was silly

September 21, 2020
Judy, King of Prussia, Pennsylvannia
Q1: 5 Brenda was very knowledgeable with what I needed. Very kind and helpful.
Q2: 5 Very satisfying

This is what I imagine Judy looks like
* not an actual Judy

September 22, 2020 Steven, Mechanicvile, New York
Q1: 1 Was told my new phone will ship the next day, still has not, on hold again to try and get this fixed
Q2: 1 Sick of this

September 22, 2020 Muralidhar, Overland Park, Kansas
Q1: 5 She answered all my questions, and provided the right services.
Q2: 5 Good service

September 23, 2020 Susan, Carthage, North Carolina
Q1: 5 Brenda was knowledgeable, friendly, and resolved my issue.
Q2: 1 I am bothered that resolving my issue took a customer service call.

September 24, 2020 Pinchus, Worcester, Massachusetts
Q1: 5 She was nice, friendly, courteous, professional, confident and knowledgeable!
Q2: 5 A nice employee does it for me

September 27, 2020 Willie, Del Norte, Colorado
Q1: 5 Very pleased with custom service rep help
Q2: 5 Change last rating to 3. The last time I called Randomcorp before yesterday, rep didn't give me all info I needed

September 27, 2020 Zaicha, Cortland, New York
Q1: 5 She was knowledgeable and friendly
Q2: 4 The wait time is too long. I understand it's under staffed due to Covid 19.

SURVEY SAYS!, CONT.

September 28, 2020 Janet, Grand Rapids, Michigan

Q1: 5 She was very polite and took the worry away

Q2: 5 I'm happy with this

September 28, 2020 Lynette, St. Petersburg, Florida

Q1: 5 Representatives of Randomcorp speak English, Yay! Very helpful with getting our new service working.

Q2: 5 She is very personable, took her time with us, as we are technologically challenged.

September 29, 2020 Travis, Sterling, Colorado

Q1: 1 I don't have time to wait on hold. I'm tired of wasting my time with this. The rep didn't give me my credits and I shouldn't have to pay fees. I've been with this company for years and don't deserve this treatment. Start appreciating you're [sic] customers

Q2: 1 Randomcorp is a scam and I'm tired of getting screwed over by your stupid idiot retard reps. Start hiring employees who know something and can figure out how to give me what i want or im leaving [sic]

September 29, 2020 Raymond, Lincoln, Nebraska

Q1: 5 She was very pleasant and helpful

Q2: 4 The automated payment wasn't helpful, Mary helped with complete satisfaction on my end. Not everybody likes to use autopay, there are people in this world that still like to talk to a real person.

September 29, 2020 Derek, Mt. Vernon, Indiana

Q1: 1 Dumb cunt

Q2: 1 I pay too much and wait on hold too long

September 30, 2020 Soo-Yun, LaJolla, California

Q1: 5 Very pleasant and helpful. Seems interested in really helping customers. A godsend these days

Q2: 5 Reliable company

September 30, 2020 Diego, Garden City, Kansas

Q1: 5 She was polite and pleasant great communication and excellent service

Q2: 5 Because it's a fact

September 30, 2020 Dimitar, Baltimore, Maryland

Q1: 5 Mary proved OUTSTANDING. She is obviously highly trained, professional and easy going

Q2: 5 Good experience

Ding dong

September 30, 2020 1:22 p.m.

Oscar from Wyoming, Ohio with questions about his bill. I tried to explain the charges but I could hear someone in the background yelling out more questions. Oscar paused and told me he was going to put his wife on the phone.

A woman with a thick German accent came on the line, introduced herself as Ana and started yelling at me. She demanded to know what this charge was about and where this charge was coming from and how did this get on her bill. She made me do the math over and over and she kept yelling at me because she didn't believe I was doing it right. Actually, I wasn't doing any math. I was just reading the numbers off of her bill. She yelled a lot. An elderly German woman yelling at you for thirty minutes is no joke. When she finally realized that I was right and that her bill was actually correct, her mood did a complete 180. She became overly friendly and acted like the last thirty minutes of verbal abuse never happened.

She forgot to hang up the phone after we stopped talking. I could hear her walking away singing "Ding Dong the Witch is Dead" in German.

Call log

7:01 am Susie from Lipan, Texas set up a payment arrangement. Her husband was in a car wreck and could not work.

7:20 am Michael from Jamaica, New York was trying to call the UK. He also told me that he is tired of being on lockdown and wants his freedom back. I told him, unfortunately, I was not able to assist with that. I did, however, provide the correct dialing code for the United Kingdom.

7:25 am Melissa from Armonk, New York needed help activating an old phone until she could get to a store.

8:14 am Patricia from Mount Carmel, Pennsylvania needed to change her due date and was worried that her ex-husband was hacking her phone.

8:20 am Richard from Decatur, Indiana called in to lower his bill. When I changed his plan, I accidentally deleted everything in his cloud storage.

8:52 am Marc from Pageland, South Carolina needed more high speed data on his mobile hotspot. He let me know that even though he smokes, he can still run two miles in 15 minutes.

9:25 am Debra from Chapel Hill, Tennessee called about her order. I messed it up then panicked and transferred her to another department.

9:48 am Thomas from Linden, New Jersey made a payment arrangement.

9:55 am Sherry from Jasper, Texas made a payment arrangement.

10:03 am Sandra, from Tacoma, Washington needed a return label to send back her phone.

10:24 am Latoya from Dathan, Alabama reported her husband's phone lost.

11:36 am Renee from Yemassee, South Carolina made a payment arrangement.

11:40 am Luis from El Paso, Texas asked if his phones were unlocked so he could sell them.

AUGUST 13, 2020

12:06 pm David from Pleasant Grove, Utah complained that his phone has too much stuff on it.

12:24 pm Egil from Yorba Linda, California reported his son's phone lost.

12:34 pm Susan from Queen Creek, Arizona called about her bill. She was very passive aggressive, but no match for me.

12:54 pm Charles from Pleasantview, Tennessee is waiting for a heart transplant and is having technical issues with his phone. He is very nervous he will miss the phone call if a transplant heart becomes available. His bill also has some errors. He is a nervous talker. His wife died two years ago from cancer. He has an African Gray parrot who said "Where are you going?" when they took his wife out of the house in a body bag. I sent him a phone. He was really nice.

1:42 pm John from Denver, Colorado paid his bill.

1:47 pm James from Sale City, Georgia made a payment arrangement.

1:53 pm Lynn from Frankfort, Illinois called to disconnect her son's phone. He died last month.

2:13 pm Shelley from Tuscumbia, Alabama filed an insurance claim for her son's phone.

2:25 pm Davis from Naples, Florida was a crabby blind man from the Carribean. I eventually got him to joke with me and I ended up giving him a credit that was too high because I am not that great at math.

2:51 pm Blanca from Winterpark, Florida was upset that she hadn't received her prepaid Visa cards yet. She said that "this has actually damaged my relationship with my husband." She said that she did not have food and that she needed to use the prepaid card for medicine. She also said her husband left her over this issue. I was probably not as sympathetic as I should have been.

Heavy bre

The typical day on the Randomcorp customer service phone lines is usually really busy with back to back phone calls. Customers often have to wait on hold a long time… sometimes up to an hour or more. This makes them understandably cranky. It's a relief when we're slow, but there is a trade off. That's when the perverts call in. They never have the stamina to wait on hold for an hour just to jerk off.

We get random pervs and we have our regular pervs. All of our regular pervs block their caller ID. Every now and then I get an amateur who forgets to do this and I usually call him back, say hi and ask him if he needs any other help with his Randomcorp account. He gets flustered, freaks out and hangs up. I just want him to know that I know he's pathetic and has failed at being a competent pervert. I put most obscene callers on hold and then see how long it takes our horrible hold music to, I presume, kill their erection and hang up. I used to try to make fun of them or goad them, but that just encourages them. They're just looking for a female voice to jerk off to, so the more I talk, the more material I give them. I figure switching them over to our hold music has got to be a boner killer for anyone. I've only had one caller who made me really, really uncomfortable. He was sociopathic-sexual-predator-type creepy. That call stuck with me for a couple of days.

Our regulars pervs have been calling in for over five years and, for the most part, use the same story every time. They're not limited to call center or geographic area. I've talked to female reps all over the country and they've all had the pleasure of dealing with these guys. Below are some of our Super Stars...

Baby Oil Guy

Exactly what his name suggests, he's always "just reaching for the baby oil." Somehow after calling in five years, he still hasn't reached it. Unimaginative perv… the worst kind.

I Missed the Bus Guy

This guy starts off the call asking for the phone number of a Randomcorp store near Kansas City. Then he launches into a story about how he missed the bus or got kicked off the bus. He will tell you that he was supposed to get on a bus that day but his ride didn't get him there on time or something grievous happened and he got booted off. He asks if you've ever been kicked off a bus. He'll mix it up by talking about various bus companies. He just keeps talking about different scenarios where he's stranded without a bus ride… keeps talking and talking. Every time you try to bring the conversation around to Randomcorp business he will ask for store information again - because he knows he has to have a shred of a legitimate reason to keep you on the phone - and then go back into tales of missed busses. All the while he's just trying to keep you on the phone long enough to finish jerking off.

One time he called and as soon as he asked for the number of a store in Kansas City, I knew exactly who it was. He said, "Guess what happened to me today?" I replied, "Did you get kicked off the bus?!" He went silent for a good five seconds and hung up. I finally felt like I won.

Hiccup Guy

Similar to "I Missed the Bus Guy" but talks incessantly about hiccups. He talks about how much he hates the hiccups and what things he does to try to get rid of the hiccups and asks you if you've ever had the hiccups and what you do to try to get rid of the hiccups. He just keeps you talking and talking and talking… about the hiccups… while he's getting off. For over five years he's been masturbating to hiccup talk.

Toe Nail Polish Guy

This one's not too exciting. Average foot fetish guy who calls in and talks about painting toenails, what kind of toenail polish you have on, asks other random questions about your feet. Maybe he could give the I Missed The Bus Guy a ride...

Belly Roll Guy

This guy calls in and talks about his "big, white belly" and how he wants to "rooooooolll!" What he lacks in creativity, he makes up for in enthusiasm.

It's a sad commentary on

September 3, 2020, 1:22 a.m.

Scott from Richmond, Virginia called in with questions about his first bill from Randomcorp. He was shocked that he was expected to pay activation fees and was concerned that he didn't see the discount for using autopay. I reminded him that he had agreed to pay the activation fees when he started his service with Randomcorp. He replied in a mildly outraged tone, "but I don't pay activation fees. I'm not supposed to pay those."

I tried to distract him with something more positive, something shiny… I reassured him that once he enrolled in autopay, he would get the autopay discount and he would even get a double discount on his next bill to make up for the missed month.

"I suppose I'm going to have to call in and jump through hoops to get that discount next month," Scott said.

"No, it's automatic," I reassured him. "It will be on there and you won't have to do anything." I told him that he just needed to set up autopay and he would be good to go. He could set it up online or I could transfer him to our automated system to enroll.

Apparently this was asking too much of Scott. It was far too much work for him to do and he told me that I was going to do it for him. He ranted about the nerve of us expecting him to waste his time (again) jumping through hoops to get the discounts he was entitled to. Why should he have to do the work? It was ridiculous. I would've gotten around to offering to set up autopay for him… but he really needed to tell me how important it was that I do it instead of him. So I got his payment information, put him on hold and entered all his information through our automated-talk-to-the-robot-lady-system, a daunting task that took all of two minutes.

When I was done and came back on the line with Scott and he asked me if I had "taken care" of the other charges. I told him that I could credit half of the activation fees - $60. He was not happy but after complaining awhile, he begrudgingly agreed.

After I issued the credit, I explained to him that I couldn't manually credit back the taxes associated with the upgrade fees, but they would be automatically credited back on his next bill. "Yep, taxes," he said, "gotta pay Uncle Sam for all those people who don't want to work." I paused and couldn't make words for a bit. After thirty minutes of Scott complaining about the outrages expectations Randomcorp was placing on him by asking him to enter his own payment information online, I didn't know how to respond to his comment about work ethic. Instead I just changed his credit from $60 to $20.

While I was making the adjustment, Scott went on and on about how I was the best customer service rep he's ever had. He said that I was incredibly professional, friendly, easy to work with and easy to understand. I hadn't told him about the reduction in his credit. The condescending praise went on some more and then he said he hoped someone was listening to the call (i.e. so some Randomcorp official would hear his valuable feedback). I don't think he really cared if I heard what he was saying. It didn't seem like it was for my benefit. I just laughed really hard and said that if I was the best customer service rep he's ever had, then that was a sad commentary on contemporary life. But I don't think he was paying attention anymore and he hung up.

Oh Helen...

September 26, 2020, 2:22 pm

Helen from Stockton, California was upset because configuring our equipment required her to use an electrical outlet in her home that was saving for "other purposes..." She ranted about this for over ten minutes while I stared at the ceiling. Once she started wrapping up, I thanked her for calling and wished her a good day. She replied, "I will never have a good day now. Not after this disaster."

"I will never have a good day now..."

Call log

7:00 am Margaret from Sharon, Massachusetts made a payment arrangement.

7:07 am Tammy from Laurel, Mississippi called about a phone she returned. She had not received her refund yet.

7:38 am Jessica from Toms River, New Jersey called in for technical help with her iPhone. While we were troubleshooting, her phone's Siri starting saying "cat pee" over and over. We couldn't get it to stop until she turned the phone off. I ended up transferring her to Tier 2 Tech Support. I wonder if they fixed the cat pee problem or if it's happened again.

8:03 am Myles from Little Elm, Texas needed the log of his text messages.

8:22 am Denise from Greenville, South Carolina told me that we have to trust in God and that it shall be revealed.

9:24 am Kyle from Ramsey, Minnesota was whiny about our prices.

9:33 am Helen from Moline, Illinois called in about her bill. Her grandson had ordered a phone and messed up her account. Every time I tried to explain it to her she interrupted me and talked over me. After twenty minutes of getting nowhere she got an incoming call from the hospital and accidentally hung up on me when she was trying to put me on hold. I called her back and finally sort of explained the issues on her account. When I was done, she condescendingly said, "Well, good job! You worked really hard for me today. I just opened a bag of candy bars. If you were here today I would give you one. You should be proud of yourself! Good job!"

10:07 am Barbara from Clarksville, Indiana got laid off and asked about discounts.

12:02 pm Charles from Dickinson, Texas called about a late fee.

12:08 pm Alphonso from New Hope, Minnesota was really nice but kept asking for random credits. I told him no over and over. He said, "That's okay. I'll just call back tomorrow and see what they can do."

10:11 am Charles from Herndon, Virginia called to report a scam call. He didn't want me to do anything, just wanted to warn us. He seemed like he just wanted to talk to someone. He said that I "empathized well" with him.

AUGUST 18, 2020

11:31 am William from Harrison, Michigan was having technical problems with his phone. He told me he is a retired police officer with a traumatic brain injury. He has problems with his short term memory and he couldn't remember what tech support told him to do to fix his phone. He didn't like going to his local store for help because he said it was run by jackasses. I offered to help him but he said he would just forget. He mentioned several times that he needed to get to the VA for an appointment but kept forgetting. I called the VA clinic for him and transferred him to Kelly at the VA Call Center. I wasn't able to help him with his phone, though.

12:31 pm Pedro from Gary, Indiana broke his phone and didn't have insurance. I got the impression he believed me and felt like I knew what I was doing.

12:50 pm Allison from Hamburg, New Jersey called to transfer her daughter's phone onto the daughter's boyfriend's account.

1:02 pm Dan from Newburgh, New York called about transferring his 85 year old sister's ipad onto his account. According to Dan, his sister was not very tech savvy. He was very condescending when he talked about her. He told me he was 78 so he knew how to handle things and was up to speed.

1:20 pm Doug from Alexandria, Tennessee called about his bill and then we started discussing issues with his service. He said that he has spoken with our tech department several times and he knows he's in an area with poor coverage. Cutting down some trees on his land would help, but he just won't do that. The trees are an integral part of his spiritual well-being. He asked if he could do a quick Reiki healing session on me over the phone. I told him that I really wasn't supposed to discuss non-Randomcorp business. He encouraged me to call him once my shift was over so we could "pick up where we left off." I did not call him back.

2:05 pm Myron from Wellsboro, Pennsylvania called to transfer his phone onto a business account.

2:21 pm Sarahlee from Eureka, California called to start a new line for her sister.

CALL LOG, cont.

2:32 pm Shane from Madison, Wisconsin was obnoxious and flirty. He sounded like a 20-something, entitled, white guy. He asked me for my number and said he was very disappointed that I had a boyfriend. I don't have a boyfriend. But when he asked me if I was married I said no, and then he said, "Well you must have a boyfriend." I didn't say anything. I tried not to say much. He was gross. He asked me for my number. I hate being nice to customers like that.

2:44 pm Sean from Scranton, Pennsylvania had questions about getting a phone for his 13 year old daughter. The call dropped but he didn't answer when I called him back.

2:47 pm Randy from Columbia, Missouri kept saying "Yes, dear" to me in a tone that sounded like he was talking to his wife with a heavy layer of condescending exasperation.

2:59 pm Gene from Washington, D.C. was trying to port out his phone number to a competitor. I'm supposed to try to "save him" - get him to stay with Randomcorp. But instead I gave him all the information and made it extremely easy for him. I even transferred him to the other company. Because life is really hard right now so what's the point of making things harder. Something should be easy.

3:10 pm Laura from Webster, New York started off the call being really condescending and passive aggressive. I needed a number off of her phone and she insisted on reading it to me four digits at a time so I wouldn't get overwhelmed. When I gave her some technical information, she said "Well, now that's not my understanding. How can you prove to me that that's accurate, Mary Beth." Then her phone started working. So I guess I proved it was accurate.

---

welcome back to

my happy place

more things I look at so I don't want to die

Chickadee - this was my grandma's nickname for me

It doesn't mean they like you

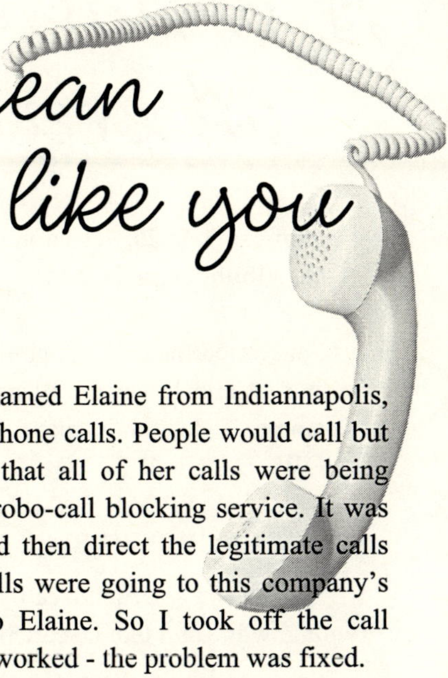

September 29, 2020, 2:24 p.m.

An older, African American woman named Elaine from Indiannapolis, Indiana called because she was missing phone calls. People would call but her phone wouldn't ring. I figured out that all of her calls were being forwarded to some number owned by a robo-call blocking service. It was supposed to filter out the spam calls and then direct the legitimate calls back to her phone, but instead all the calls were going to this company's number and none were coming back to Elaine. So I took off the call forwarding, tried calling her phone and it worked - the problem was fixed.

Elaine told me about a time in 2011 when she lost service with her landline phone for over a week. She said it was part of a conspiracy involving an "enemy neighbor" who knew someone who worked at the company who provided her landline phone service. She wasn't able to contact 911 or get ahold of any help. This was before she had a cell phone so she was left without any form of communication.

"You have to be careful,' she said. "You might have a neighbor that becomes your enemy. And they'll say, 'I don't like the way she looks, I'm going to find out her name and mess with her phone."

She said it didn't matter where you were. "My parents always told me, 'Just because someone acts nice doesn't mean they don't want to hurt you,' so every time you're at the grocery store and someone smiles at you it doesn't mean they like you. They might decide to follow you out to your car so be careful."

If I had this conversation with a white person, I would've thought they were crazy. But this reminded me of how scary it must have been, and still is, to be non-white in America. How much energy it must take just to be in the world and survive.

Elaine was so happy and grateful. She had been in a panic because she cares for her adult daughter with special needs and depends on having a

continued on page 34

I know where you live

September 7, 2020, 7:15 a.m.
Kyle, Albuquerque, NM

I answered the call in a chipper voice, "Hi this is Mary Beth, may I have your first and last name please?" The customer answered "A Pissed Off Customer." He didn't take a breath, just went straight into a rant about "HOW DARE WE LOCK HIS PHONE?!! HE PURCHASED IT DIRECTLY FROM SAMSUNG, RANDOMCORP NEVER OWNED IT…" * Rant!* Rant!* Rant!*

This was my second call of the day. The customer, "Kyle" sounded young, white and like he called customer service a lot.

I calmly told Kyle I would be happy to unlock his phone. As I went about doing this, he went on and on about how horrible we are, how bad our customer service is, how much he hates our automated answering system and how EVERYTHING ABOUT RANDOMCORP IS JUST WRONG AND MAKES HIS LIFE MISERABLE! I had problems unlocking his phone, but I didn't tell him that… I figured I could reach out to our tech department once I got him calmed down a bit.

I asked Kyle if he was enjoying the recent drop in temperatures, casually mentioning that I also lived in Albuquerque. I wanted him to know that I know where he lives. This seemed to calm him down a little and the call turned into more of a chat than a one way screaming rant. He told me that he had just gotten off working the graveyard shift as a security guard. Twenty-something white male security guard… of course.

Kyle let me know that he had pre-ordered the new watch from Samsung. He asked me to send him a sim card so he wouldn't have to call us back to activate it when it arrived in the mail. I told him that since the Samsung watch had a non-removable sim card that comes embedded in the watch, he did not need one. Because the device doesn't require a sim card, our system won't even allow me to order and ship one to him. He was not pleased with that answer and insisted I was

wrong. I let him know that I would love to do what he was asking, but it was not necessary or even possible. He continued to enthusiastically insist that I was wrong saying that Samsung told him he needed a new sim card from us. "ARE YOU SAYING YOU KNOW MORE THAN SAMSUNG?!?!!" After several minutes of yelling, I put him on hold and tried to figure out a way to order any type of sim card for him, even though I knew it wouldn't work in his watch and even though I knew he didn't need it. I just wanted to get him to shut up and go away.

Apparently the time Kyle was on hold gave him a chance to recharge all his white-male-entitled-frustrated-security-guard-whatever rage. When I came back on the line he started shouting, "YOU DID NOT UNLOCK MY PHONE LIKE I ASKED YOU TO AND YOU CAN NOT DO WHAT I WANT! HAVE YOU DONE ANYTHING? ARE YOU EVEN WILLING TO DO YOUR JOB AT ALL?"

I tried to tell him that I was going to reach out to tech support, but he said, "NO! I WANT YOU TO FIX IT! It's your problem, now you have to fix it. You messed it up, now do your job. Or are you capable of that?"

At this point his level of anger and self-importance was so ridiculous it was hard not to laugh.

He started going on again about how we waste all of his time every time he calls and how he just ends up filing complaints with the Better Business Bureau and on and on and on.

I suggested that in the time we've been discussing the situation, I could've had tech on the line and the problem would've been resolved. He did not appreciate this perspective.

He started shouting that he was going to report me to the Better Business Bureau. He asked me for my employee number and I told him I don't give that out for security reasons. So he asked for a reference number for the call. I made up some random, super long, meaningless number… probably 40-50 digits long. He repeated it back to me twice to make sure he had written it down correctly. Then he spent the next ten minutes demanding to speak to my supervisor to report my performance. He only needed to ask once, I would've transferred him in five seconds to get him off the line.

After I got a supervisor on the line, I muted my phone and listened in. She told him exactly what I told him. He yelled a little then told her he would file a complaint with the Better Business Bureau and hung up.

A lot of customers threaten to file complaints with the BBB, but this customer has actually done it. He's done it so many times that our Corporate Communications Team (the top rung on the "I want to talk to the manager" ladder) sent him a letter stating, "...just as we never want our customers to be harassed or treated with disrespect, we expect the same treatment from our customers towards our representatives." From looking at the account history, it seems like I got a pretty mild version of Kyle. He was particularly cruel to some of the other representatives. I haven't heard if I got my own Better Business Bureau complaint yet. I'm on the lookout for security guards named Kyle in Albuquerque, New Mexico.

continued from page 31

reliable phone in case of an emergency. She asked me if we could accept tips, because she wanted to send me some money, maybe by PayPal. She said she would give me a hundred dollars because she was so relieved.

I didn't know what to say. This lady was amazing and all I did was click a button on a computer and hit enter. I told her no, this was my job and I was just glad I could help. I thanked her for being a customer and wished her a good day and blah, blah, blah. After she hung up, I logged off my phone and sat there awhile just being grateful.

I have no illusions that the few interactions I have like this make my job one of service to humanity. I work for a huge, evil corporation whose priority will always be profits. And everything I do is supposed to further that goal. I feel guilty about this. But getting to talk to people like Elaine makes me feel better, even if I know I'm mostly just deluding myself. But, eh… I'm still grateful for calls like this. They help take the edge off of being a tiny cog in the giant wheel of late-stage capitalism and all that.

Nobody's listening to you

OR THINGS I DO WHILE ON A CALL

Even though I'm at home, I remain tethered while I work. I still use the standard company issued corded headset. I could splurge on a fancy wireless bluetooth headset but I like the challenge of finding activities I can do within a ten foot radius of my desk. Here are a few of my most recent diversions (ranked in no particular order).

1. Cut my toenails
2. Fold laundry, usually towels
3. Try to draw better pictures of swans
4. Try to communicate telepathically with my dog
5. Plan my future cult
6. Disinfect all the surfaces around me
7. Research ways to repel and discourage pigeons
8. Pay bills
9. Make various themed spreadsheets
10. Fill out online gift registries
11. Correspondence - digital and analog
12. Owls
13. Name my plants
14. Send miscellaneous print catalogs to people who annoy me
15. Draw temporary tattoos on myself with Sharpies
16. Create alias email accounts
17. Make lists of places I want to visit (then compile information into spreadsheet, see above item 9)
18. Cover various items in wood grain contact paper
19. Sign up for free trial offers and trial subscriptions
20. Cancel free trial offers and subscriptions before I'm charged for anything
21. Cyber stalk
22. Write manifestos
23. Watch YouTube videos of dogs herding sheep (preferably Border Collies)
24. Organize my desk drawers
25. Tape and/or glue things together

Call log

7:00 am Luis from Gainesville, Florida called to reverse his last payment and make a payment arrangement for next week.

7:08 am Robert from Silver Lake, New Hampshire called to disconnect his father's phone. His father died last week.

7:37 am Kenya from Trenton, New Jersey made a payment arrangement.

7:49 am Lindsay from Millington, Maryland wanted to see if we could lower her bill. She was laid off due to Covid.

8:06 am Frank from Toms River, New Jersey asked about a feature on his phone. He was funny and had a dark sense of humor.

8:40 am Lois from Brookline, Massachusetts thought I was a telephone operator. She let me know that she's 93 years old and kept referring to me as "Operator." "Thank you, operator." "Yes, operator." "Operator! Can you hear me?" "Have a good day, Operator." I transferred her to the department she was trying to reach.

8:48 am Paul from Pasadena, Maryland called in to pay off his phone so he could move his phone number to another carrier. He said he just had to get away from the madness. At his age, he could not take the madness of Randomcorp anymore. No. He was done.

8:58 am Ryan from Crete, Illinois called because his bill was incorrect. He was really nice and not confrontational.

9:20 am Rory from Gilberts, Illinois thought we should send him a free iPhone because he has been a customer for ten years. I wanted to tell him that there's no such thing as a free iPhone.

9:44 am Kelly from Biloxi, Mississippi called in and said her bill was too high. She kept yelling and saying that it was just too high. I tried to ask her questions so I could help her but she would not answer me. She just kept talking and talking and yelling. Finally I yelled at her and told her that I couldn't help her if she wouldn't let me talk or ask a question. She stopped talking and hung up. I did not call her back.

10:21 am Ann from Euclid, Ohio wanted to get a hold of her son's call logs.

11:30 am Valerie from Cozad, Nebraska wanted to disconnect her service. I grew up in a small town 75 miles from Cozad. I also photographed the

Cozad Wastewater Treatment Facility one summer in college when I was working as a photographer for an engineering firm. My photos were published in one of the firm's promotional brochures. I did not share any of this information with Valerie.

11:43 am Sandra from Montgomery, Alabama called to check that her phones were insured because her grandchildren were constantly losing or breaking them.

12:02 pm Daniel from Beacon, New York called about his past due bill.

12:09 pm Gilbert from Wolf, Pennsylvania called because his mom’s phone was not working. I could hear a toilet flush in the background.

12:23 pm Thelma from Bolivar, Missouri called to check on a promotion. I could tell by her voice that she didn’t believe me.

12:50 pm Stephanie from Virginia Beach, Virginia called about her bill.

1:20 pm Rusty from Mesa, Arizona called because his account had been disconnected by Randomcorp corporate headquarters after he made death threats at his local store. He said if I didn’t reconnect his service, he would die.

1:57 pm Robert from Peculiar, Missouri called about his bill. He tried to be passive aggressive but he was just not very good at it. He kept dropping hints saying “I guess I’m just going to have to go to another carrier,” or “I’ve been with Randomcorp for ten years, and I really hate to leave…” He probably said something like that at least ten times. He was also angry about the stocks he had in the company. He started off the call being an asshole and it frustrated him that I didn’t respond. I was just quiet, let him rant and drop his hints. I didn’t say much. He eventually talked himself into being satisfied with his Randomcorp account. He was falling all over himself apologizing to me for being rude earlier, saying “It’s not about you.” I didn’t say anything. They always say, “It’s not about you.”

2:23 pm Michelle from Webster, Texas called to make a payment arrangement. She told me she was a sixty year old Asian woman and had come to America in 1975. She had been out of work for four months due to Covid. At the end of the call she told me to “Take care, God bless, wash your hands, stay safe and have a beautiful life.”

CALL LOGS, cont.

2:38 pm Jorge from Farmington, New Mexico called in to get a return label.

2:41 pm Wendy from Cottonwood Heights, Utah was irate because she had been auto-enrolled in paperless billing. She was furious that we were taking away her choice and she said that making her go online to view her bill was putting extra work on the customer. She kept ranting that the whole policy was ignorant because the energy used to cool computer servers is just as bad for the environment as printing paper bills. And on top of all that, our hold time was unacceptable.

3:02 pm Catherine from Kokomo, Indiana was 72 years old and ended the call by saying, "You have a good day, babe!"

3:10 pm Sarah from Pittsburgh, Pennsylvania called in about her past due bill.

3:17 pm Allen from Billings, Montana called to check on his order.

3:24 pm Michelle from Wilkes-Barre, Pennsylvania called in and immediately began screaming that her bill was wrong for the third month in a row and that she could not continue to live like this. She started crying and told me that she was supposed to be painting her new office, but instead, she had to call Randomcorp because we had once again fucked up her bill. She ranted some more and then told me that I was the reason people commit suicide.

Tiffany's anus...

September 9, 2020, 9:24 am

Tiffany from Macon, Georgia was upset about her bill. Particularly, she was outraged that we charge less per line the more lines you have on your account - a volume discount. Tiffany only had one line, so she said "So you're telling me I'm just getting f-ed in the bootie?" (She didn't say "fucked," she said "f-ed") I tried to explain the reasoning behind the pricing. She then replied,

"So I have to take it in the anus?
All in the anus. In my anus."

But Josie calls me Lori...

September 13, 2020 2:45 pm

Josie from Baltimore, Maryland called in for help to get her call logs from the current bill cycle. She accidentally deleted the call history in her phone and she needed to find proof that she dialed a certain number for court the next day. She said she had been meaning to do it but she kept forgetting, so she just HAS to get it done now.

But first she needs to know how to send a copy of her bill via email. Josie sounds young - under thirty, at least under forty. I should not have to explain this to someone that young. And they should not get angry when they don't get it. I have no problem teaching 80 year olds how to do this. I realize that I sound a lot younger than I am, but c'mon Josie. After fifteen minutes, she finally emailed a pdf file of her bill to her friend, Wendy. She called Wendy just to make sure. I spoke with Wendy a bit.

Back to the call logs... I show Josie where to find them on the website. She was using the browser on her phone which has limited options. She said she didn't know if it will be admissible in court. I told her if she accesses it from a computer she can download an excel document or pdf... but apparently this isn't an option for her because her laptop isn't working. She wasn't able to log onto this morning's church service on her laptop, so how is she supposed to log onto her Randomcorp account? I don't know what I was thinking making such a ridiculous suggestion.

So I offered to try to download it and email it to her. I'm technically not supposed to do this. It's a big stretch and a pain to do it with the tools I have access to. But whatever, at this point Josie is the bigger pain. I download it, format it and email it to her.

Josie opens the file... "But it doesn't have my name and number and blah, blah, blah… and I don't know if the judge will like it… and what's the point of even doing this if it's not even going to work blah, blah, blah!" So I do it again… customizing it to the exact specifications preferred by a judge in the state of Maryland, according to Josie.

And all this time, all of these 53 minutes, she has been calling me Lori. Near the beginning of the call she stopped and asked, "What's your name again? Lori?" I told her no, it's Mary Beth and she said, "Oh well, Lori works..." and I was Lori for the next 53 minutes.

Call center job performance is measured almost solely by a set of predetermined metrics. If your numbers are good, you are a good employee. It doesn't matter what you sound like on the phone - if the numbers are high then you're doing great. I'm a prime example of this. My numbers have always been higher than what you would expect if you listened to me handle a call. When I was still working in a physical call center and co-workers could overhear my end of a phone call, they were shocked to discover that my performance ratings were so good. Some of this was due to my Midwestern self-deprecating modesty, but it also reflects my uncanny ability to look great on paper and be a mess in real life. I'm one of those innocent looking, sweet sounding white women who never has her receipt checked when leaving a store. Although, for many years, someone really should have been checking… but that's a whole other story.

Randomcorp tracks a whole slew of things... how many customers cancel their service, how long we spend on each call, how many calls we transfer to another department (or, in my case, transfer to some other random company). They tally up our survey results and how closely we conform to our schedule. That's right, no 17 minute breaks tsk, tsk, tsk. A big part of our performance is based on how many customers call back within a certain amount of time. The less people who call back after two, five and thirty days the better. We want to solve their problem the first time they call and make sure they never, ever have to call us again. Our goal is to make our jobs obsolete and the better we are at advancing that mission, the bigger raise and bonus we might get... I try not to think about it as I have few truly marketable skills.

Every year they adjust which metrics count towards our performance score. Some years it works better for me than others. For example, I am a born people pleaser so I do well at customer satisfaction, but I feel like asking someone to buy something is too pushy, so I'm not so hot when it comes to revenue generation. Generally, I'm just as shocked as everyone else when my numbers are high. Up until the last year, every call felt like a disaster, I felt like I had no idea what I was doing and I was sure Randomcorp would finally discover my incompetence and fire me. But then came the plague and they mercifully stopped measuring our performance for most of 2020. That's when I finally started to like my job. It was a beautiful thing not to care if the asshole yelling at me for the last thirty minutes was going to give me a bad survey. And if a nice old man called who reminded me of my dad, it was okay to talk to him for an hour, nobody was counting. I know Randomcorp will start measuring our performance again. This party can't last forever. But in the meantime, I've started tracking a few metrics of my own.

Please note, this data is not collected in a fashion that could be considered remotely scientific. It is statistically meaningless. Almost all of this information is volunteered by customers. It is not my habit to ask, "Are you still paying for your adult child's phone?" or "Did your adult child who lives 1,000 miles away buy you this iPhone, tell you it was going to be easy to use and now you can't even figure out how to call them and complain about it?" No, these figures are strictly recreational. I like to record information and organize it into attractive looking charts and/or spreadsheets. It's very calming and really takes the edge off of a stressful job.

Please turn to page 42 to take a gander for yourself...

Cookies for homeless people

September 28, 2020, 8:32 am

Sharon from Toms River, New Jersey yelled and ranted about her bill and how buying a phone from us was the biggest mistake of her life. She went on to say that our company will hire "any idiot off the street" and that "all we do is fuck things up." She ranted about Bernie Sanders and Communism. She kept going on this theme for approximately twenty minutes. Then, she exclaimed that she was on the phone with us for six hours yesterday all the while she was supposed to be making cookies for homeless people. I had to mute my phone because I started laughing so hard. I put her on hold and transferred her to another department.

MORE THAN JUST A number continued

6969 PIN

The number of customers who use the number 6969 or a similar combination (i.e. 0609, 6699, etc.) as their account pin number per total customer contacts per month.

HONEY/SWEETIE/DEAR

The number of customers who call me Honey, Sweetie, Dear or another condescending term of endearment (i.e. Sugar, Babe, etc.) per total customer contacts per month.

FREELOADERS

The number of parents I talk to who pay their adult child's phone bill or have their adult child's phone on their account (and pay the entire bill) per total customer contacts per month.

NOT MAD AT YOU…

The number of customers who start their abusive verbal rant with "I'm not mad at you but…" per total customer contacts per month.

TEACH MY ELDERLY PARENT TO TEXT

The number of senior customers whose children buy them an iPhone because they think iPhones are "super easy to learn," and "It will be no problem for Mom to catch on even though she can't check the voicemail on her flip phone," per total customer contacts per month.

TGYSE! OR "THANK GOD YOU SPEAK ENGLISH!"

The self-righteous, not-so-thinly veiled racist exclamation, usually delivered in a ha-ha-inside-joke-I'm-talking-to-another-white-person way once customers learn my name is Mary Beth (that's such a *nice, traditional* name…) Gross.

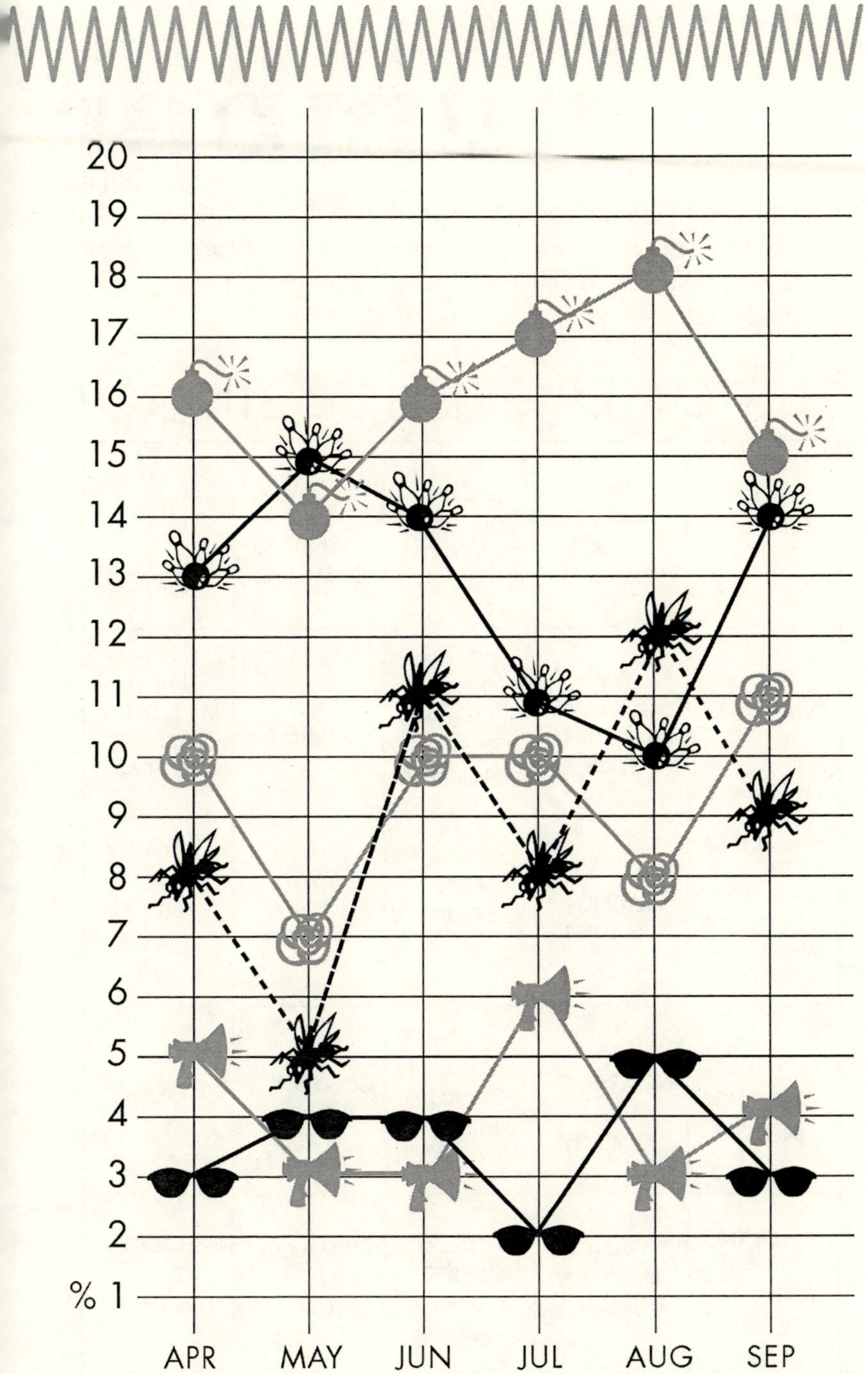

20
19
18
17
16
15
14
13
12
11
10
9
8
7
6
5
4
3
2
% 1
APR
MAY
JUN
JUL
AUG
SEP

MORE THAN JUST A number CONTINUED

Another way I make use of my collected data is with a rousing game of bingo. It's entertaining and distracts me from plotting against unruly customers.

CUSTOMER SERVICE BINGO!

"THIS IS THE XTH TIME I'VE CALLED ABOUT THIS!"	"AM I TALKING TO A HUMAN?"	"CAN'T YOU WAIVE THAT FEE?"	OLD MAN THAT REMINDS ME OF MY DAD	PERVERT
INTERRUPTER	"WELL THEN I'M CANCELLING MY SERVICE!"	"DO YOU KNOW HOW LONG I'VE BEEN ON HOLD?"	FREE LOADERS	TEACH MY ELDERLY PARENT TO TEXT
"I'VE BEEN A CUSTOMER SINCE 19XX!" (A DATE BEFORE RANDOMCORP EXISTED)	"I'M NOT PAYING FOR THAT!"	**FREE SPACE!**	6969 PIN NUMBER	CUSTOMER CALLS ME ANOTHER MARY COMBO
CUSTOMER CALLS ME BRENDA	"I'VE NEVER HAD A LATE PAYMENT!"	CUSTOMER TELLS ME I SOUND LIKE I'M FROM MINNESOTA	CONSPIRACY THEORIST	TGYSE!
"I'M GOING STRAIGHT TO SOCIAL MEDIA!"	"I WANT TO TALK TO A SUPERVISOR"	HONEY/ SWEETIE/ DEAR	"I'M NOT MAD AT YOU..."	"I SHOULDN'T HAVE TO PAY FOR THAT!"